How To Keep Them Reading

A Guide To Writing
An Engaging Non-fiction Book

Ebony Lynnel Harris

Go from idea to book while overcoming any obstacles holding you back.

© Ebony Lynnel Harris

All rights reserved. This book or any portion thereof may not be reproduced, distributed, or transmitted in any form or by any means, including photocopying, recording, or other electronic or mechanical methods, without the prior written permission of the publisher, except in the case of brief quotations embodied in critical reviews and certain other noncommercial uses permitted by copyright law. For permission, write to the author at the email below.

ISBN: 978-1-951614-10-2 (paperback)
ISBN: 978-1-951614-18-8 (hardcover)
ISBN: 978-1-951614-19-5 (ebook)
ISBN: 978-1-951614-20-1 (audiobook)

BE Publishing Co., Baltimore MD.
www.faith2faithbooks.com

How To Keep Them Reading

A Guide To Writing
An Engaging Non-fiction Book

Ebony Lynnel Harris

" Time is one of those rare commodities that you can't get back. Don't waste your time trying to be like everyone else. Choose to stand out. Be prepared for inspiration to strike at any moment. Always have something to take notes on. Some ideas don't repeat as often as we would like them to."

- Ebony Lynnel Harris

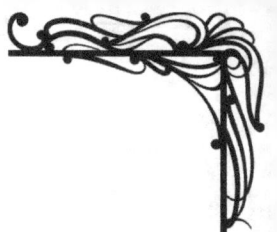

Thank You

To God be all the glory! I want to thank God for allowing me to write another book. God, you are nothing short of Amazing!

I have to extend special honor to my mom, the vessel that God used to bring me into this world. I appreciate you. Everything up to this point was designed to help me get to where I am today. I have not forgotten the many sacrifices you made for all your children.

Special thanks are due to my oldest sister Rose. You truly are one in a million. Your love for your family exceeds many others. I am grateful to have you in my life.

> *I start each book with this in mind: I am creative not because I was born with talent or acquired this skill, but because the Creator made me in His image; thus, I create. Finally, I end each book with gratitude and relief that God allowed me to finish one more book. Then with a determination to go on, I go back to my growing list of book ideas, pick one and start working. As ready writers, our cups are full not to keep it to ourselves but to share with the world."*

\- Ebony Lynnel Harris

Dedication

This book is dedicated to my son, Ethan who always cheers me on and to his facial hair that has yet to appear; but, we know it's on the way. That's right, you keep brushing your smooth face, son, until you can one day brush a patch of hair. Don't brush too hard, it might be difficult to explain why you have scratches on your face. So brush regularly, but lightly.

Yes, one day I'll have to order you one of those manly shaving kits. Not that I'm excited about your face looking like a Chia Pet, I'm building up evidence. One day I'm going to walk into the bathroom, look at the sink and ask you if that's your hair on it. Then when I tell you that I knew this day would come, you're going to think I'm joking again. I wrote this dedication so you would know, that I knew you would one day leave your facial hair on the bathroom sink, before the strands of hair ever thought to crawl out of your pores.

Yes, I know you're going to do your best to clean up after yourself after reading this. It might not be today, tomorrow or the next day, but one day, you're going to slip up and I'll have my evidence. When that day comes, all I want to hear is, "You were right, Ma." I love you son, thank you for your continued support. I'll be watching you.

Last but not least, to those of you who are struggling to get through writing your book. Remember, details are important.

> " So, you think you can write a book? You're halfway there. Fear is a liar. Fear will tell you not to try because you might fail, but the one thing worse than failing is not trying at all. Let that sink in.
>
> - Ebony Lynnel Harris

Introduction

How To Keep Them Reading
A Guide To Writing An
Engaging Nonfiction Book

Are you struggling to write a book or unsure of where to begin? Maybe you started, but now you're stuck and haven't touched your project in a while. I want you to know that you are not alone. In fact, I've been where you are.

I started writing as a young adult. I didn't have a format or outline, just an idea of what I wanted to say. It went well until I let words of discouragement create a roadblock that stayed with me for a long time. Please be careful who you let speak into your life. I eventually gained the courage to try one more time. I know how it feels to struggle with writing or knowing if your work is good enough. Can you see yourself writing a book? If you can't, I see it for you. This book is packed with helpful information to guide you through the writing process.

- Ebony Lynnel Harris

> *If the thought of writing a book makes you feel uncomfortable, relax, you're normal. After a while, it might seem as easy as a walk in the park. Even experienced writers get turned around from time to time. Have you ever been to a park and saw a sign that says, "You are here." That's what a good book outline does for you."*

\- Ebony Lynnel Harris

Table Of Contents

Thank You 5

Dedication 7

Introduction 9

Preface 13

How Do I Get Started? 15

What Is A Nonfiction Book? 17

Book Outline 39

Expanded Outline 47

Character Development 55

Rough Draft 65

Final Draft 71

Write Your Book Introduction 77

What Next? 83

Your Anchor 89

Overcoming Self-Limiting Beliefs 95

Another Way 101

The Ready Writer 105

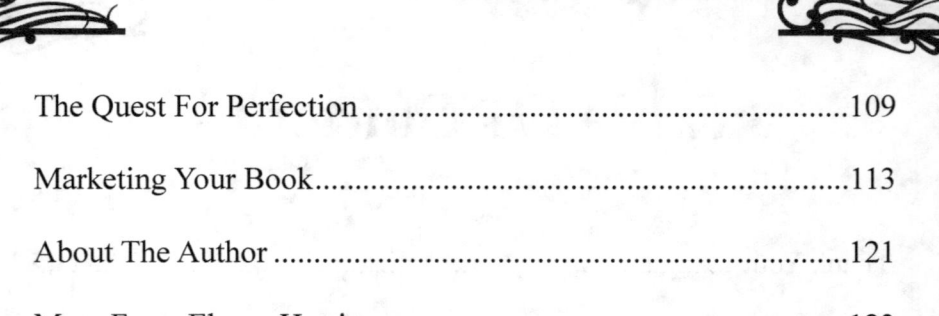

The Quest For Perfection 109

Marketing Your Book 113

About The Author 121

More From Ebony Harris 123

Preface

It's just after midnight. I'm sitting at my laptop with a dilemma and looking to solve it. I asked myself, "How can I help individuals learn how to write?" When I do workshops, I am limited to the number of people I can work with, usually by seating. Then we have those who can't sit in a 2-hour workshop in the middle of the week because of their schedules. I also have those I ghostwrite for and coach. How can I empower them to do it on their own? The last thing I want is for someone to leave this earth without utilizing what God has placed in them.

With that in mind, I get inspired and then I start writing. I'm not sure how long this will go on, but I am determined to see my thoughts through. It felt like the ideas were coming too fast to sort and type. So I took out my pen and notebook paper, wrote down my thoughts, and organized them. Not timing myself, I started with what I had, which eventually turned into a book. I had to be willing to see things through. It's now 2:00 a.m. and my rough draft is complete. I am writing some things to include in the preface for the book I started writing earlier in the editing software.

Within hours, I wrote a book and edited it a few times. I took a couple of breaks. I let the dog out to use the tree, got some coffee and ginger snaps, then I got back to writing all over again. Often, inspiration strikes when everyone else is sleeping. It's that inward alarm clock that won't let me sleep. Its sound says, "write it or lose it." I decided to write it, producing most of the book you are reading now.

Next, I attempt to come up with a design for the cover of this book. My son tells me that my first designs aren't going to cut it, and I knew it already deep down. It isn't until after 9:00 a.m., that I produce a book cover which I love, and it also gets the approval of my son. Priceless! I often write and publish my own work. Once I have finished the draft, I create a book cover to visualize what will eventually be released. I place it where I can see it, to serve as a constant visual reminder of what has to happen. I will still go over my book again and again, until I feel it's perfect. This book will go to the editor, as soon as I read it without the need to change anything.

I don't want to jump ahead too much. Let's talk! Who am I, and why am I qualified to guide you in writing your book? My name is Ebony Harris and I am a writer. I am the mother of a writer, a teacher, a writing coach, and a ghostwriter. I would not say that I'm a writing expert, just someone with a deep love for the craft and a desire to help others see their potential. I believe everyone has something to offer the world. We should share our stories and experiences, so that others might overcome their struggles.

How do you get started? The most straightforward answer to that question is, start writing. I have had the pleasure of helping individuals of all ages. The youngest student was six years old, and at the other end of the spectrum, an individual in their seventies. I keep writers of all ages in mind; with that said, the information you read should be more than enough to help you write your book.

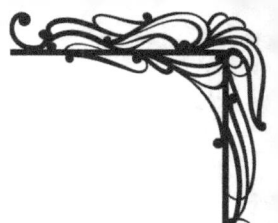

How Do I Get Started?

Have you ever waited in line behind someone who could not decide what to purchase? I have, and it's frustrating. Then, when it's my turn, I sometimes do the same thing. I hesitate because I don't know what I want to buy, and if I am ordering for someone else, that makes it more challenging; I want to make sure they like what I get. That's a lot like writing. Many may wish to write a book, but they have various thoughts going through their mind, and it's hard to pinpoint where to begin. We write for an audience that many of us will never meet, so how do you know what they need? Keep reading, and we'll get there. I know you've heard it many times, but writers read. It's just a fact.

Another thing writers do is write. Yeah, they don't just think about it; they put it on paper. I ask individuals who desire to write books but lack the discipline to go on a journey. It lasts about 120 days, and during that time, we commit to writing and reading every day. You can do this without using writing prompts. Write something every day, no matter what. It can be a blog post. Try using the notes app on your cell phone, a pen and paper, or your computer. Whatever you do, start moving forward and stay focused.

"It is the consistency of writing, even when you don't feel like it, that develops you as a writer and positions you for the inspiration which comes to those who took the time to prepare."
- Ebony Lynnel Harris

Usually, I only need to prime the pump to get my creativity flowing. One of the ways I do this is by researching, and after digging, it pours out. In case you didn't know, research is a part of writing; they go hand in hand. You want to be knowledgeable, right? As I stated earlier, many who come to me have hectic schedules. From cover to cover, a moderate reader will finish this book in roughly two hours.

What is the best way to go through this book? How should you use this book? First, read through the entire book. Next, you should go over the text and complete each section's activities. I strongly advise you to read this book before starting your writing. If you are in the middle of your project, do your best to apply what you learn from this book to your work. Finally, with your acquired knowledge, plan to write your book, set attainable goals, and follow through.

What Is A Nonfiction Book?

I know what some of you are thinking, "Is she giving me an explanation of nonfiction? I learned that in grade school, and another thing, back in my day, we used to…." Well, you get it. Yes, I am. Although you learned what nonfiction was so long ago, this is for those who may need a refresher or need to understand further. Hear me through.

non·fic·tion

/ˌnänˈfikSH(ə)n/

noun:
Nonfiction writing is always facts. It includes real events and real people. "There are many non-fiction books that help people through difficult times."

Nonfiction has many sub-genres. I'm not just talking about biographies, autobiographies, maps, history books, science, and social studies. The world of non-fiction is so much larger. I wouldn't say it's a bottomless pit, but it is pretty deep. What type of non-fiction book will you write? Let's take a closer look at the sub-genres.

The sub-genre that I help writers with the most would be the memoir. So many want to tell their stories. These stories can help others, and readers like to learn about the writer. Memoirs are real historical accounts based on personal knowledge. When writing a memoir, you are not writing about your whole life, my friend. That would be an autobiography. It would help if you focus on a snippet. Also, you don't have to write a memoir in order. You can go back and forth. When I coach individuals through their memoirs, we focus on creatively retelling parts of their life. We want to grab the reader's attention while making sure the book stays true.

One of the memoirs that caught my attention as a child was 'I Know Why the Caged Bird Sings,' written by Maya Angelou. It wasn't just a story. It came off the page and I identified with her.

Anne Frank wrote another famous memoir, this one in the style of a diary. Although she didn't know her journal would be published, 'Anne Frank: The Diary of a Young Girl' paints an accurate account of what happened to this family, while living in Amsterdam during World War II.

Numerous politicians, actors, singers and everyday people have either written or had their stories ghostwritten for them in the form of a memoir. Why? Because their story can help someone else. When deciding which sub-genre you want to write, remember, Memoirs are about a particular experience that caused you to be where you are. The experience could have been good or bad. You can even write about a decision that changed your life course.

Since I started with the memoir, it seems like the next logical sub-genre to discuss would be the autobiography. I know it sounds boring, but the thought of autobiographies like 'Long Walk to Freedom' by Nelson Mandela reminds us of how moving this sub-genre can

be. In this particular book, Mandela tells about the not so easy path he walked to become a revolutionary and the President of South Africa.

I think of the abolitionist Frederick Douglass, who wrote three autobiographies. When I opened one of his books, the front page read, "NARRATIVE OF THE LIFE OF FREDERICK DOUGLASS, AS AN AMERICAN SLAVE." When you look below the title, it says, "WRITTEN BY HIMSELF." Autobiographies don't have to be boring. Some of them are meaningful and powerful. Some of them feel like you're holding a piece of history itself.

The next sub-genre is the Expository section. Have you had an aha moment? The Expository helps us to focus on essential issues that may get overlooked. It should bring truth and awareness. One book that I found helpful was 'When Breath Becomes Air,' by Paul Kalanithi, a neurosurgeon who started to journal his cancer journey. It is a heartfelt book that helps the reader see that they too have to number their days. Some people don't start living until they realize they're about to die. If you plan to write this type of book, make sure you have a thorough understanding of your subject.

The next category in the sub-genres is the Biography. Biographies are similar to the autobiographies, but written by someone other than the author. You can write a Biography on anyone. I mean anyone! Just make sure it's accurate and don't try to tear a person down.

Some non-fiction books can go into several sub-genres. Whether it's a memoir, autobiography, biography, or expository, we aim to con-

nect with readers through personal experiences making the character, (whether it be yourself or another) relatable.

There is yet another sub-genre, which is narrative nonfiction. When I think about this category, I think of exciting, creative and compelling characters you fall in love with. I think of stories that you can relate to with details that are groundbreaking and out of the ordinary, yet it's entirely accurate.

I'm talking about books that were so good you would think they were fiction. Listen, there are plenty of good reads in non-fiction. I'm thinking of 'A Night to Remember' by Walter Lord, which tells the tragedy of the Titanic. It gave us a reconstruction of what happened on the ship. Then we have books like 'The Short and Tragic Life of Robert Peace,' by Jeff Hobbs, which tells of a brilliant young man in the prime of his life, whose education and acquired knowledge could have taken him far, instead, his choices led him to an execution-style murder. Books like these grab our attention and keep us entertained, warning us of the dangers some haven't considered.

The next sub-genre I'll mention is vast. That would be your good ole self-help or Prescriptive Nonfiction book. Think of self-improvement, self-help, devotional, instructional, or how-to. That's right; this book in your hands is prescriptive. If your aim in life is to write a bestseller, consider teaching something and you might make a bestsellers' list. The self-help sub-genre always has best sellers. That's because people have this inward desire to learn and grow. As always, research is important. Make sure you are knowledgeable of your subject and relatable.

News of a poorly written book travels just as fast as the news of one that's well written. Consider your interest in writing a book; most individuals can't afford to pay hundreds of dollars a month to a writing coach, but they can afford to pay for a book that might take a couple of hours to read. A well-written how-to-book will act as a coach. If you didn't catch it, that was a hint for a coach to pick up a pen and write.

Motivational help books are popular because many pour out of themselves daily and need someone to pour into them. So if you want to motivate, there's a market. Then we have the books on business, which is rightfully a genre of its own. Entrepreneurship has grown the need to "fire your boss." Sounds better than ever, especially in a pandemic. If you want to start a company, you need only go to your local library and find the books you need or purchase them at book stores or online. When I started learning how to publish books for my son in 2012, the library was where we started. One of the things I told him was, "You can learn anything from a book, but most people don't take the time to read and find out."

Are books of poetry nonfiction? Well, yes and no. It depends on the subject of the poem. When they talk about the author's life or another's life, some are classified as literary nonfiction. In any case, it's a heated debate on where poetry falls. A lot of the poetry that I've heard and read is real. It talks about the things the poet went through like memoirs or autobiographies do. They help to raise awareness on issues frequently overlooked, like an expository. Poetry can be prescriptive and motivational, assisting individuals through tough times in life. Although the debate continues to go on, I can't rule out poetry as nonfiction.

In nonfiction, it's alright to leave something out as long as it is not essential to tell the story. For example: Don't write a book about how despicable a person was for a crime they were accused of when you know someone else confessed to the crime. If you find yourself wanting to write nonfiction and you don't want to share relevant information about your life, or you want to switch things up a bit, consider writing a fictional novel based on a true story.

One of the questions I get a lot is, "Can I get sued for writing a story about my life?" Well, yes and no. Sometimes it's not what you say, but how you say it. I keep stressing this, make sure everything you write is accurate and not based on opinion. We don't intentionally try to harm people with our writing. If your book has lies that can negatively affect the individual's livelihood, yes, you can be sued for the lie. It is called slander.

You can write a fiction book based on a real story, but nonfiction always contains truth. It should not have part of the truth and part lie, that would be fiction. You made it through this incredibly long definition of nonfiction, I tried to exclude it, but I couldn't. For your reward, You now get to do an assignment and apply what you've learned. I know you're rushing to thank me, so why don't we jump into our first assignment of this book. I hope you're excited about the possibilities!

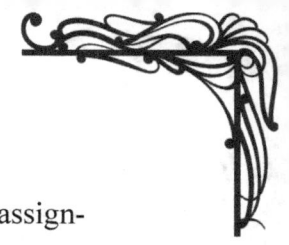

Assignment #1

Alright, It's time for the long-overdue, highly anticipated assignment. For this first task, you're going to decide what kind of book you want to write.

Do you like to talk about others and the things they did to change the world? Consider writing a biography. Do you want to bring something to light that keeps getting overlooked? Write something in the expository sub-genre. Do you want to tell your own story? You can write an autobiography, an expository, or a memoir-style nonfiction book. Maybe you want to teach or motivate and inspire the world. The key to remember is that nonfiction should be accurate accounts of what happened, how things are, or how to accomplish a matter.

So, what sub-genre of nonfiction do you want to write? It's a simple question that takes a lot of consideration. I caution you, although, after time, writing becomes a walk in the park, that park includes hills and hurdles that change depending on the sub-genre and story. All of them require research and hard work. In this book, we go over techniques to incorporate in your writing to keep your readers focused on the message you want to give. Do you want to speak on a matter, raise awareness, or give praise? Poetry might be an option for you. Although the poetry genre is too vast to include in this how-to book, I have two words of advice for the poet, full transparency. It will make a difference.

Is it hard to figure out what style of writing you want to use? What do you love to do? What gets you excited? What do you feel drawn to do in life? How can your experiences help others? Friend, it's hard to write about something that doesn't interest you. If you don't feel connected to the contents of your writing, how can your reader?

The Effective Storyteller

Let's walk through what makes a compelling storyteller. Do you have a message that you are passionate about sharing? Maybe you want to share your experience or knowledge to bring about change. If you walked into a crowded room, who would you talk to, and why? How would you relate to them? Why would they be attracted to you and what you have to say? It helps to consider these questions before you begin writing. You don't want to finish writing and find that it's not written in a way that connects to people. Even if you have a divinely inspired word, you need to know how to relate to individuals.

Think about who your audience will be. You have to write in a way that will catch their attention and keep it. One way you can connect is through empathy. We can reach a person faster, if they feel we can relate to where they are, what they are going through, or what they have endured. A method that I use is to include first-hand experiences in my writings. As children, we learn to love stories and we subconsciously put ourselves in the place of the characters. Likewise, your readers are searching for a connection to the content they are reading. Give it to them. It is the emotional connection that will keep the reader engaged. A good book will cause the reader to laugh, cry, get excited and have a wide range of emotions; emotions that are directly attached to the memory. If you can get a person to connect emotionally with your book, they will not forget it. They will read it repeatedly, because the connection spoke to them.

You want your book to be easy to understand. No one wants to keep looking up the definition of words every time they read something. That goes back to knowing your target audience. We read not only to learn, but also for entertainment. Writers today have to compete with movies and advancements in technology. I've seen movies that were so well put together, that I was in awe at the special effects. You would think with all this technology, that our minds would be advancing along with it. The reality is, it impairs the imagination. You can fill a book with information, and no one will read it. After a while, it becomes tiresome, like a chore. For your writing to stand a chance against motion pictures, you can't just say it. You have to help your audience see it! As a writer of the 21st Century, our responsibility is to help our audience exercise their imaginations, which is powerful.

Have you ever had to force yourself to read through books with lots of technical stuff? Textbooks give you information, not entertainment. Keep that in mind when you write. Your book can't be compelling to me, if I'm not interested in reading your message. It also goes back to personal habits, as a writer. As storytellers, we read a vast variety of writer's materials and develop a standard - an ideal writer image that we strive to be with each piece we write based on the books of others. Thus, consider what you are reading.

I caution you, don't get so deep that you force your readers to fall into a state of confusion. Take the time to research this on your own; the average American adult reads below a 12th-grade level; most of them are closer to the eighth-grade. If you want to appeal to a broader range of readers, simplify your writing. You can use an online editor that detects grade levels. The editor I use has a setting called "General"; this setting helps me to see if my writing is easy to read with minimal effort. My fourteen-year-old writes books that can be read and enjoyed by the "average" American adult. I tell him to keep writing and keep reading, that's my advice to you. Future authors, a book that is at most on an 8th-grade reading level, may sound less sophisticated to you, but in the long run, if you write by the tips in this book, you will hold the attention of more readers because they can understand you. We talk more about online editors in later chapters.

Assignment #2

When I am working with a client ghostwriting or coaching, this next step is always the same. I ask them to write out a book summary. I hope you came to the table with at least an idea of what you want to write. Write between two and four paragraphs describing your book. You will use this as a guideline to make the writing process go smoothly.

Know Your Audience

How do you respond when you know someone is watching you? It might not bother some people, but for others, it can determine how you will act. The same applies to writers. When writing for myself, I relax a lot more than if I were writing for someone else. As a ghostwriter, I am always cautious about what I present to the client. Rough drafts for my clients are not as 'rough' as the drafts I write for myself. You may not be ghostwriting for a client, but keep in mind, you are writing for someone. You may not know them yet, but eventually someone needs to read what you have to say.

Now that you have completed your book summary, decide who your audience will be. Don't wait for your book launch to determine your target audience, that's much too late. Benjamin Franklin said, "If you fail to plan, you plan to fail." Think about the type of people you want to reach with your writing. When my son wrote his first book at six years old, people would ask him which age group his book was for, and he would reply to them, "My book is for everyone." As writers, we want everyone to read and enjoy our work, which is highly unlikely. I can't write a Christian book and expect someone with contrary beliefs to keep it on their bookshelf; that's wishful thinking.

Assignment #3

Let's build reader profiles.

For school-aged individuals, I encourage you to write to your peers. (Parents can help younger children with this activity, until they can do it on their own. Don't be afraid to help with spelling, editing, etc.; you are your child's biggest cheerleader.) These exercises will help them learn to write better in general.

Others, I encourage you to write addressing a small group of anywhere between three and five individuals. All of whom are unique and represent a group you are trying to reach. Give each person an identity. You may want to give each person a face to have a visual representation of your audience. Below are possible questions you might want to ask yourself, while building your profiles. Try not to make your audience too similar. Think diversity. You want to describe at least three groups of individuals who need to hear the message you are saying.

(Use the questions below when building a reader profile. Ask questions relevant to the type of book you are writing.)

What problem do they want you to solve?
Are there references you can use that they will easily recognize and understand?
What issues are they facing?
What are they interested in learning?
How can you add value to their lives?

(Create questions of your own)

Friend, I have to give you some sobering news. When writing, always remember that your book is not about you. Readers tend to place themselves in the story. As I stated earlier, we learn how to see ourselves in the words we read at an impressionable age. It gets baked in, and it sticks with us. Thus, we are always looking to see ourselves in every story. What has your experience taught you that they could learn? Can you offer a glimpse of hope or help someone find courage? If you intend to meet a need, you, my friend, are on the right track to becoming a nonfiction author. List the possible needs or concerns you can address in your book and seek to do so.

> *Finding your book's audience is a lot like math. We are not counting people, but looking for the most significant common factors. It's not about their age or gender, but the issues they need you to address. Identifying those issues will lead us to our audience."*

\- Ebony Lynnel Harris

Book Outline

There is much debate on how to write a book. Everyone does what works for them. When we talk about an outline, you might run into an experienced writer who will tell you they sit down to write and keep going until a book comes out. They don't need anything to keep them on track. A person like myself has so many book ideas going through their mind that they have to keep writing everything down. I can work on more than one book at a time because I create outlines for each book. Yes, my mind is intact, and I can stay on track. Having a detailed outline for each project is the key. I don't advise you to work on more than one book if this is your first book.

Also, don't overthink it on the word count. If you choose to self-publish, a book between 10,000 and 20,000 words is acceptable. Kindle makes becoming a self-published author easier than ever. One can always go the traditional way of publishing, but be prepared to write a lengthy book.

Your outline is your map, guiding you to your goal of finishing your book. Writer's block is a problem for many; however, I don't experience it when I plan correctly. I believe having a plan eliminates the guesswork because you shape what you were going to say in the outline and expanded outline. With all that writers do to produce a book worth publishing, having a book outline allows for fewer snags. The last thing you need to deal with is writer's block.

Many may experience what they believe to be writer's block. During my time coaching, I find that it's one of two things. On the one hand, you don't know what to write and where to get started. You start writing and get stuck, not knowing what to say. The first step in writing your book is knowing what to write. My friend, if this is you, you are not experiencing writer's block. Your struggle is called uncertainty. To overcome, figure out your message. In the end, it's all about your readers and what they need. Ironically, I found out "wants" don't always equal "needs."

On the other hand, you failed to plan appropriately. Thus, unsure of where your story goes next, you run into an issue, the dreaded writer's block. Friend, this does not have to put a halt to your writing. My rule when ghostwriting or writing for myself, unless I can outline the book from start to finish, I don't start writing the book. Sure, I may have to add or subtract a few chapters, but I have established the desired outcome and a route to plan and achieve it. The book outline briefly walks you through what each chapter is to contain. The expanded outline breaks down each chapter guiding the writer through talking points coherently, allowing one to direct their readers on a journey, this quest to acquire knowledge.

I remember when people used to print out driving directions to get from one place to another. You had the option for an overview that gave you major transitions (simple book outline) and a detailed version (expanded outline). For those who are unsure of which way to go, the detailed summary works best. The directions are straightforward, guiding you to your location. Friend, if your expanded outline does this, you won't experience writer's block.

Now that some of the preliminaries are out of the way let's get into the writing process. I often say, as a way to remember this method, to be a good storyteller, you have to think selfishly, "It's all about the ME's and the MI's, or major events and minor events. Major events keep the interest, and minor events keep the story flowing.

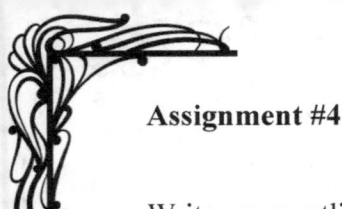

Assignment #4

Write your outline. (For this assignment, you will need standard index cards or notebook paper.)

Now, let's outline your book. What are the major events or ME's that will happen in your book? On the unlined side of your index card, write a ME's. One ME per index-card. If you can see it in your mind, that's half the battle. Start at the first Major Event, read it aloud, and go in order. Can you see how your story is shaping? This will be your book outline. If your book is about information, you can still do this exercise; you need to write the main thoughts and supporting details. (ME#1 = Chapter 1; ME#2 = Chapter 2; and so on.)

I like to do this with index cards just in case I have to rearrange details. Next, we will move on to minor events or the supporting details. Write all the supporting information or minor events that lead to this particular major event on the lined side of the index card. Major events don't just happen; there are always smaller events that lead up to them. You may want to use some lined notebook paper instead of index cards if you have too many MI's. Remember, you are not writing your book right now, just an outline, so the supporting details do not need to be lengthy. Do this for each page or index-card, and your book outline is almost complete.

(Extra Exercise: Try watching a film, not one of those low budget films. Observe and locate major and minor events. After finding the ME's and MI's in the movie, arrange them in order. Can you see how

it comes together? Watch as many movies as you need to get the writing pattern to catch your audience's attention, try reading a good book. Did the author use a similar method? If you are a minor, make sure it's all right with your parents to watch the movie you selected.)

Example

Let's look at the story, "Little Red Riding Hood." If I were to divide this story into ME's, I would pull out events that helped the story transition into the next scene. We start with Little Red Riding Hood (our protagonist) at home. It's essential to paint a picture of your character's reality at the beginning of the story. In this case, the protagonist is loved by all and views the world through her innocent eyes. I would list the first ME as the protagonist getting sent on an errand. Remember, it changed the story's direction. Our protagonist will no longer be sitting at home.

ME: Little Red Riding Hood gets sent on an errand.
ME: Little Red Riding Hood gets approached by the wolf.
ME: Little Red Riding Hood leaves the path and gets lost.
ME: Wolf goes to grandma's house.
ME: Little Red Riding Hood meets the woodcutter.
ME: Little Red Riding Hood makes it to grandma's house.
ME: Woodcutter visits grandmother.
ME: The Lesson

We dig a little deeper in the next chapter with our expanded outline. I hope you are excited about your book. I am!

Expanded Outline

You may feel like your book outline is complete, and it needs nothing else. Just know we only completed the shell. It still needs much work to be deemed an effective outline. Now, we look at our ME's and MI's to see what should go in each chapter. For each ME, list an emotion that you want your readers to feel when reading that chapter (you can have more than one emotion for each chapter). Do you remember talking about researching? Here is where you get to conduct research. I know, it's exciting! We live in an information age; everything is at our fingertips, you can do the research you need on most cell phones.

Research is vital for nonfiction because your story has to be accurate. Observing is also a part of the research process. I remember sitting down and watching as the wind blew through the trees, trying to envision words to describe what I saw. While writing my poem, "A Beast Called Grief," I took note of my son hiding behind things to catch me off guard and scare me. As a ghostwriter, I often ask my clients to describe their surroundings; observation is research. If you want to become better at descriptive writing, try people watching.

Assignment #5

Research any topics needed. List related accounts or anything you feel will help move the story forward. Don't repeat yourself. Each thought should be complete and accurate. You don't want to write down an incomplete idea and come back later, unsure of what you were saying or why. When I write, the expanded outline section is where I do the most research. It's best to research early in the project to better forecast how long this book will take. Also, you want your reader to walk away with as much value as possible. I generally complete my research chapter by chapter until I get to the end of the book.

This process will vary depending on how deep you want to go into the subject. Make as many notes on that chapter as possible, and keep it organized. Don't try to write your book at this point. Right now, you are putting together the information in a coherent manner. I rarely word information the same way that I wrote it out in the expanded outline.

In many cases, I was trying to write it before I lost the thought, or if I am ghostwriting, I was taking information as fast as I could. There have been times when I wrote something or researched something in one chapter that I had to move to another one later. Take time to get this done. Remember, the more research and discovery you do, the better your book will be.

Example

In the last chapter, we covered how to write your basic book outline. We also vaguely outlined Little Red Riding Hood. In this chapter, I'm going to walk you through how I write out the minor events in a way that helps me move forward in the story. Considering what I just mentioned, I don't think, "How do I build this expanded outline?" The thought is more like, "How do I plan this story?" Although this is a fiction story, those who are writing memoirs should take notes. Children's stories catch our attention for a reason. Let's dig in.

ME: Little Red gets sent on an errand.

MI: The scene starts with Little Red (the protagonist) at home playing.
MI: We learn of Little Red Riding Hoods personality.
MI: (Introduce mother into the story.)
MI: We learn of mothers personality, and the protagonist is called into the kitchen by her mother.
MI: Mother carefully gives instructions while packing the basket.
MI: Mother tells her she has to make it to the house by sun high.
MI: Mother warns her to stay on the path.
MI: The protagonist leaves out on her journey and starts following the road.

We are in the first scene with two characters and the mention of another. How were they introduced? What do we learn about them? Little Red Riding Hood will be our guide to help us see what our

stories can look like potentially. Disclaimer: The version I write will be different from what you normally see, because I'm the writer.

Let's take a look at the first scene. Remember, we start at Little Red Riding Hood's home. She may be inside doing what she usually does. We know her to be this innocent child with no sense of how the real world can be. At some point, she has to go on a journey. It seems simple, yet this isn't the only journey she goes on.

(If you want extra practice, list the MI's for the other ME's given in the last chapter. Walkthrough, each scene, and the journeys Little Red Riding Hood could have experienced. The possibilities are endless.)

In our stories, we want to walk our readers through journeys that touch the senses. The journey can be physical or mental. Include things your readers may struggle with from time to time. Remember that list we made earlier where I asked about your reader's struggles?

When dealing with the mind, you can have many struggles at the same time. One can struggle with thoughts of past abuse, peer pressure, low self-worth, hopelessness, unforgiveness, fear of failure, and suicidal thoughts at the same time. When we display flaws in our characters, it is not for the readers to wallow in self-pity, but for them to understand, others have been where they are and to give them a glimpse of hope. Use your reader profiles as you plan out your expanded outline. I have had books I worked on where I had more than twenty MI's in a section, and many of the chapters I write or ghostwrite can be 3,000 or more words.

Application:

How do we want the reader to apply this story to their life? We want the reader to see that the world isn't as innocent, and there are many dangers that we should be looking out for daily.

Research:

When you are writing your ME's and MI's, you don't have to go too in-depth. In this section, let's look at what we might research if we were rewriting this story. After listing out the minor events in order, I go to each section and list things I need to explore. I also outline stuff I might need to clarify. Let's consider scene 1.

ME: Little Red gets sent on an errand.

POSSIBLE RESEARCH QUESTIONS:

How old are my readers?
How can I word this to grab their attention?
What are my protagonist interests?
What is the mother like, how can I make her memorable?
Does the mother have any internal struggles?
What is the protagonist dealing with socially, emotionally, mentally, and physically?
What does sun high mean?
(Go through the story and write down every question that comes to your mind about this story.)

POSSIBLE INTERNAL STRUGGLES OF THE PROTAGONIST:

Social: She may not have many friends.

Emotional: If she stays at home a lot, she may feel the need to be accepted.

Mentally: When we look at the traditional story, we see that she struggles with being obedient and focused. Later in the story, we add our protagonist's (main characters) struggle of getting lost, regret, and anything else she could have experienced due to her decisions.

Physically: The physical journey, getting lost.

Character Development

When some people think of nonfiction, they think of books with helpful information, which is true in many cases. What about the Memoirs? If you are telling a story about your life, do you need to develop characters? Yes, for your book to be successful, you need memorable characters. When writing a book about your life, decide what you want to share with the world. I'll say it again, nonfiction is true, so make sure you always give real accounts in nonfiction. When introducing characters into the story, it's good to give a little background and help your reader see why they are there. The way you bring characters into a narrative can mean the difference between a good book and a somewhat alright one.

After deciding what you want to share with your reader, determine which struggles would best help your readers with whatever they are going through. Saying the right thing at the right time is priceless! Do you want your reader to feel empathy for the main character? Tell of some of the things they endured to get to where they are. Do you want your reader to be in suspense? Try holding back information until it's needed. Internal struggles can include beliefs or views, struggles with a set of defined morals or ethics (outside), struggling with going against the conscience (inward guidance), fear and the dreaded "What if..." Then there is a struggle dealing with shame and disappointment. I'm not saying make insecure characters. Spread these thoughts out. Help the reader see your character's thought pat-

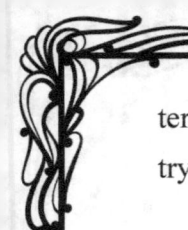

terns. Your readers may share some of your struggles, so give it a try.

I think now would be a good time to choose how you plan to tell the story. Are you good with writing out conversations? If so, you may want to tell a story. When writing out a story, make it gratifying. Your readers want to see it unfold. Do you need help with writing out the dialogue? Consider telling the story like you would if you shared it with a friend. You can also talk from the perspective of the teacher. Most entrepreneurs choose this tone, they learned something and their focus is to give you that information. What happens if you use more than one style? It can work. When I write, It's usually a mix between the conversational and lesson tones with a few stories along the way.

If you've gone through a challenging experience, have you gotten closure? When we write from our pain, we spread the pain. When we write from a place of victory, we empower. Readers can feel the emotion behind what we write. Words are spirits.

Assignment #6

I often get books to review and a common flaw from authors attempting their first book is their lack of memorable characters. The reality is some of the descriptions are so vague that it can be anyone. Now, if you're planning your memoir, remember, some of the people who read this book know you, so make sure the character you write about sounds and acts like you. Are you funny? You better tell some jokes in your book. Are you a serious person? Let us know by your tone. Are you laid back? Show us.

All of your readers won't know how you look. Unless you plan to make a picture book, you have to help them see what you are saying. It's always nice to start with a physical description. What characteristics stand out? How do you/they act? When we are talking about individuals who may have hurt us in the past, be mindful of what you say about them. Words spoken/written out of season can put a bad taste in the reader's mouth. If you want people to feel your pain and cry with you and for you, then a memoir might not be the best place for that.

I can think of a few stories that honestly say that some funerals were more exciting than they were. We don't want a monotone book. If you have a sad story, sprinkle some laughter throughout it. Even if you feel your life was the worst, I'm sure someone made you smile. The best characters are complicated, so show the many sides of who you are. You are not your situation and you are more than the limitations placed on you. Don't be afraid to step outside the box. There's plenty of room out here.

You might say, "I'm normal, and I don't do anything out of the ordinary." That can be true, but what are you thinking? Where does your mind go when it's time to relax? What are your fears and some of the things you want to do in life? What goals are you working towards completing? How has dealing with struggles affected you mentally? What is it that you do to maintain? How do you act socially? Are any of your characters loud? Does food fly out of their mouth when they talk? Don't tell me that a person always has food stuck in their teeth. Tell me about when you had a conversation with that individual, and your eyes couldn't avoid the meat stuck between their teeth. Tell me about how you inwardly cheered them on as their tongue kept rolling over it in an attempt to wash it away. When characters come into a scene, you show who they are to avoid the typical rundown that readers grow tired of hearing book after book.

In this assignment, plan your characters for your story, make them memorable. We want to fall in love with them. We want to view them as down to earth instead of distant.

Character Development Checklist

Do my characters have depth?

What about your characters draws people to them? Pages are flat, so the character doesn't have to be. Don't tell us. Show us who your character is.

Keeping it Real!

Will your characters be so perfect that no one can relate to them, or will you expose their flaws? People aren't looking for perfection but connection. So often, we get the two confused, don't miss the point in your story.

Driven

People flock to individuals similar to themselves. What drives your characters? Do they have dreams for the future? What are their goals outside of the main storyline?

Show different angles

It's unhealthy to let situations consume us. Ensure your readers can see a detachment from the situation and what's going on around your characters. The individual struggle is only a fraction of what happens in life, yet our choices play a huge role.

Passion

Does the protagonist feel deeply about something? Add contrast to what the antagonist cares about as well. Your readers want to know the characters.

Battles
What are the battles your characters are fighting? Have they run into resistance? What does the opposition look like for your characters?

Relatable
Will your readers be able to see themselves in the characters?

Strengths
What are your characters' strengths? FYI, if this is a memoir, you shouldn't be the only one with strengths. You may not see it as harmful, but that says a lot about you, so look for the good in others. It might take some digging, but it's there.

Internal Struggles
Remember, we have layers, so let's not focus entirely on the outside layer. Is there a struggle between goals, morals, etc.? Go deeper.

Consequences
What are the consequences of the choices your character will or may make? While some are unforeseen, others help us to see the situation as a whole.

Sacrifice
What are the sacrifices to be made? Does this affect the story?

Choices
Every day we have choices. Displaying a character's nature can be as easy as walking your readers through events revealing how they perceive things.

Transformation

Will your characters change during the story? In what way? Will any circumstances lead to that change?

This list is in no way exhaustive, but it will help you to dig deeper to evaluate what you plan to write.

(You can go to Faith2FaithBooks.com for additional writing aids.)

> *Superheroes aren't the only ones with backstories. Everyone has a past. Sure some of them are boring and will have you going to sleep, but some of those backstories will have you sitting on the edge of your seat waiting for the next word. That all depends on who's telling the story. Memoirs are better with backstories. It helps your readers walk in your shoes."*

- Ebony Lynnel Harris

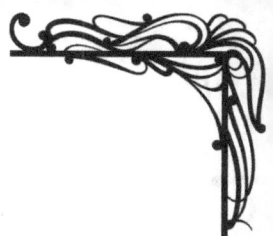

Rough Draft

Finally, it's time to start working on the draft of your book. If any anxiety tries to arise, remember you have a guide to keep your writing on track. You have your expanded book outline, which is one step below a draft. Use your research, the ME's, and the MI's to guide readers in the way that you will have them to go.

You have identified your target audience and can imagine the faces of some of the readers. Focus on the issues they need you to address. Write as if you are speaking to them, be direct, talking as if they were standing in front of you. Entertain, enlighten, and attempt to help them through their problems. Now is the moment you've been waiting for; write your book.

The reason I divide chapters by the ME's is to ensure my story does not plateau. Tell your story, progressing it at a steady pace. Are there any quotes or phrases you can put in your book that speak to your readers? Connect with them emotionally? What personal experiences will you include? Ask questions to connect with your readers. You want them to feel you wrote the book for them. Many of them will answer the question in their minds without even realizing it. Paint a picture with your words; using an idiom or two, you can be witty and, at the same time, amusing. When you strategically add figurative language to your writing, it will pull your reader into the story and engage the senses.

When doing the rough draft, think about what you plan to write. Will this information have your audience engaged, inspired, uplifted, revived, or captivated? What are your plans for the reader? Will your story produce that outcome? If you can answer yes to all your questions, your book is good enough to go through to the next stage, but not before going over it one more time, from start to finish.

When I write the rough draft, I usually use an online editor to write out my books. You can find many online editors at reasonable rates. Most editors evaluate your manuscript to determine the level of editing it needs. They then base their quotes accordingly, and if you weren't aware, good editing is not cheap. Online editors take manuscripts that require heavy editing and turn it into something that may only need light editing, thus dramatically reducing the cost your editor will charge you. I do not advise you to send your book to print without putting it in an actual person's hands for review. Make sure your editor has excellent references. There are some errors the online editor won't catch. Also, you don't want to lose your voice. If you put your book in the wrong hands, it will sound like someone else wrote it when you get it back.

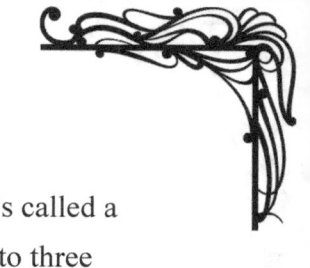

Assignment #7

For this assignment, write out the draft for your book. It's called a rough draft for a reason. Some writers break the story into three parts, the beginning, the middle, and the end. The issue comes when the reader has to wait too long to experience an emotional connection. Reading should not be a chore. In the method we are using, we follow the ME's and MI's, addressing each one until all major and minor events are listed. If I find that I don't have enough information to write about the ME I am working on, I combine it with another ME, making it and the other supporting details one of the MI's. Make sure everything lines up. Also, use a mix of sentence formats and lengths throughout your book to make it more interesting. When using short sentences, you create emphasis.

Take time and meditate on various parts of your book, exploring the depths of what you are saying in your mind. You may feel tempted to release your work, thinking it's perfect after this. I advise you to take a break and come back to it in a few hours or maybe even days. I go through many drafts each time, meditating on my book's contents until it transforms into something more meaningful. Once I fall in love with my writing, I know it's ready for a little more editing. I meditate on my work, always exploring the "what if," thus I am still editing until I submit it.

“ Have you ever completed a rough draft so perfect that it didn't need editing? Divinely inspired and without flaw, perfect in every way. It's pretty standard for me. I usually let it sit for a few days, and upon return, it's hard to find the perfection in what I initially wrote. Our divinely inspired messages get written through vessels subject to error. I'm speaking from experience. Give yourself that extra time to get over the awe of creating. It's nothing like a little time away from your work to keep you grounded. You may need it. Try not to be away too long."

- Ebony Lynnel Harris

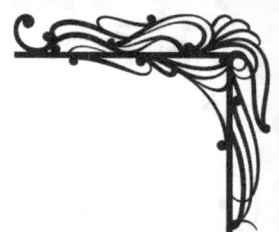

Final Draft

I usually go through many drafts before I go on to the final draft. I write, take a break, and rewrite. I can't stress this enough, and you will appreciate this process in the end. Also, you can't rush a good book. I know you are thinking about becoming an author, and you want it like yesterday. Let's go back to our audience. Remember, we created a visual on them. You may be itching to release your book. However, think about your readers. Wouldn't they want quality? Do you want to give them anything less than your best?

Writing and rewriting are essential to producing a quality book. I often receive more revelation during this process, and sometimes I see some things I initially said wouldn't work. After rewriting for a while, if I read my text and connect with it emotionally, it's a keeper. That frequently doesn't happen for a while. The story somehow unfolds over time, and it's gratifying. As a writer, you need to be able to rethink and rewrite your book. Remember, this is not about how fast you can get your book published. It's about your audience and the quality they deserve.

You must learn not only to practice but also to anticipate rewriting eagerly. If you find rewriting to be a bother, examine your connection with what you are writing. Do you feel excitement or obligation? When you have too much responsibility, the last thing you want is an extra chore. Get excited, be passionate about what you are writing. It will come together.

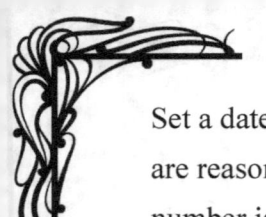

Set a date to finish your book and stick to it. Make sure your goals are reasonable, don't say that you will write for 6-8 hours a day. That number is exhausting just thinking about it. Start small, you may want to give yourself an hour or two each time. Don't set overwhelming goals. If you do, you may find the years going by while you have not started your book.

Assignment #8 - 999

Write and rewrite your assignment until each word resonates with you. Give details, be accurate, grasp, and retain the reader's attention. Your aim should be to fall in love with your writing, do this, and you will have achieved a piece worth publishing. Don't write what you can't explain. If you find it hard to connect with any part of your book, consider reworking it. You'll know when the connection is there.

> *Many first-time authors treat the final draft as if it were a quick pitstop on their journey. Instead, it should be more like an awkward goodbye where you know you have to go, but you're just not ready. Friend, fall in love with rewriting, anticipate it, develop a connection with your writing, and don't leave until you know it's time."*

\- Ebony Lynnel Harris

Write Your Book Introduction

You completed your book. Congratulations! I'm not going to ask you to summarize your book or write another outline. I find it best to write introductions after I finish my final draft. Remember when I said to write a good book, you have to think selfishly? It's the exact opposite when you are looking at the book introduction. My nonfiction writer friend, don't make this section all about you. You can mention yourself, but this better not sound like a resume. If your book made it through the book cover test, the introduction plays a crucial role in readers purchasing your book. People look at the introduction to find out what they are getting, not who you are. My advice to you is not to hold back. Let them know precisely what they will get from reading your book.

Do you remember when we painted a picture of our readers and why they needed to hear what you have to say? Considering what they are going through, you are going to speak to how they may be feeling. Talk directly to your ideal readers, and let them know that you have them in mind. In my book introduction, I tell my readers that I can help them write a book, not because I know it all, but because I've been where many are. Never underestimate the power of your past fears and failures. When you overcome, it helps others to see that they can overcome as well. Can you offer a solution to your reader? Let them know it in the introduction.

You don't always have to have an introduction to grab attention. Looking at the first chapter, what does the first line say? Is your first

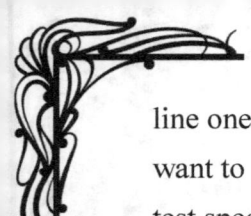

line one that makes readers want to keep going? If not, you may want to consider rewriting it. You could always use beta testers to test specific parts of your book or the entire thing.

Assignment #1000

Another way to look at your introduction is like it's a sales page. Have you ever heard of the thirty-second elevator pitch? Your goal is to pitch your book in under 500 words. 'Emphasis on under 500 words.' My introduction is only 155 words, yet it tells the readers exactly what they are getting. I know you just finished writing your book, you may be tired of writing, but now is a time that you don't want to skimp. Put your best foot forward, and make an excellent first impression. Whatever you do, don't fill the introduction with random, unconnected thoughts. Let everything have a purpose. Are you an authority on a matter? Solutions and results are much more useful than credentials. Consider your potential reader's level of reading, and speak so they can understand you. Above all else, be yourself. Authenticity is important.

> " There's a place in every book to bore readers to sleep; it's the 'About The Author section.' You, my friend, can cure someone's insomnia and strategically place your resume for all to see there. All other areas, including the book introduction, should be engaging."
>
> - Ebony Lynnel Harris

What Next?

You finished your book and the book introduction. Now you want to submit it for publishing. Should you log on to KDP (Kindle Direct Publishing) and submit your book? Now, I want you to take a deep breath; breathe in and out. Then, imagine me running to you, grabbing you by both shoulders, screaming while shaking you back and forth, "Don't do it! It's not worth the risk!" Do I mean that it's not worth the risk financially? Maybe, you have to consider what you want to make from each book. In any case, the chance I'm referring to is submitting a book that hasn't been beta-tested. Two things that your book needs after its completion are beta readers and editors.

I know your whole family read your book and told you it was good. They may not have wanted to hurt your feelings. When I submitted this book for beta testing, I got a three-page report back on this book that addressed my concerns about my book and gave me advice on what to add to my book to make it a better read for you. Remember when I said I was trying not to do a definition of a nonfiction book? It was suggested and seconded by a beta reader and the editor. I know I can be lengthy in my explanations, pray for me. So what is a beta reader? A beta reader is a person who will read through your book and give you an honest opinion of it. Do you have questions? You can ask them, and they will tell you in their report. Not all beta readers put forth the same effort.

A beta reader can be a volunteer who likes to read and provide feedback on books. Initially, I chose individuals I knew who were more informal, but when I went with a professional beta reader, that's where I got the three-page detailed report. I was like a kid in a candy store. Testing a concept or product is nothing new. Larger companies use beta testing to perfect their products all the time. Have you ever tried a product in the beta stage? Consider your book as if it were a product because it is. Your friends and family might not be as thorough as a stranger would. I even have beta testers for my online courses. Why? Because beta testing works.

I know you want everyone to purchase your book, and you don't want to give anything away, but for most individuals, beta testing can drastically improve the odds of your book becoming a bestseller. Having multiple beta testers can tell you how the public perceives your book and if anything was hard to understand. I know I keep going back to it, but the best beta readers would be the ones in your target audience. What better way to get feedback than to ask the ones you are trying to reach. Make sure the individual you plan to ask will be honest with you. Then you want to make sure you get someone who can commit to the task of reading. If a person keeps your book sitting for weeks, how is that supposed to help you when you may have deadlines? While family and friends show up for you in a crunch, I found hiring a professional beta reader to be worth it in every aspect.

I like to have at least one reader for each person represented in my target audience. When you are talking about paying, I know that it can get a little costly, but it is worth it. The beta readers I paid for have been worth it.

In planning this book, I sent out my information to a few friends and family and kept getting excellent reviews. Then I sent it to a few beta readers, and it was as if one of the beta readers I chose went through this book with a fine-tooth comb holding nothing back. She was honest, finding things that I didn't consider a big deal. She suggested that I define nonfiction, which made sense after hearing her out. Each time I received advice, I would think about what it meant to my book. I changed my book several times. How long will you need to keep your book in the beta stages? I would keep it there until I can have someone read it without the need for significant changes. I found beta readers that I love, but I will give my work to another beta reader to have fresh eyes and a new perspective on my work each time.

What do you need to do before giving your book to a beta reader? Maybe you won't hand your book to an editor first. They do charge a nice amount of money. I think it is common to use an online editor to edit any documents before sending them. When it comes to online editors that help you check errors while writing your work, I have my preference. Yet, because I don't want to endorse any one product, I would say, go to your search engine of choice and type in, "FREE & PAID ONLINE WRITING EDITORS WITH PLAGIARISM DETECTION." You may be saying, Plagiarism? Yes, It's a real problem. Many of us say quotes, and we don't even realize what we are saying. We think it's a common phrase when we should properly cite the author.

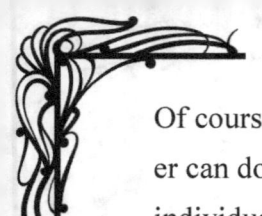

Of course, what I gave you was only a snippet of what a beta reader can do. Many of the beta readers I use are experienced writers and individuals who have a love for reading. Some of the individuals classified as beta readers are what we would call alpha readers. They are authors and individuals who work in the publishing industry who bring to the table a wealth of knowledge that can help you when publishing your book. Any genre can benefit from beta or alpha readers.

Your Anchor

Again, I have to ask why 'YOU' need to write 'THIS' particular book? What is unique about the message you are telling? We can get inspired to do things and then stop because we feel inadequate. Maybe you think no one will receive your work or that you are unqualified. When doubt tries to speak to your mind, it can sometimes outshine the initial joy and excitement about writing. I just gave you a formula for how to write that repeatedly produces results. You may be excited right now, but what happens when you run into an issue? Doubt can arise, but it doesn't have to stay.

It's not the fact that you know what you have to do that holds you to your responsibilities. When you realize why you are doing it, that keeps you anchored even when you feel like you can't make it. Write down your book goals. One of the reasons I take the time to design a book cover early in the process is to give myself a visual reminder of what is to come.

Why will you stay committed to writing this book? Encourage yourself. No matter what, don't stop progressing. Set your goals to keep going until it's finished. Maybe you need someone to hold you accountable, who will encourage you along the way. Don't let fear hold you back; you never know how far you can reach if you're unwilling to try.

When doubt comes inwardly, we sometimes strive to reach an undefined seal of approval from our peers. It always leaves you questioning yourself and your worth. A mark that I have yet to obtain. Something that helped me overcome this dilemma was determining that I would no longer write for people's approval but God. In turn, my writing became more transparent, and what others thought about my work meant little to me. It wasn't for them anyway; they get to share what I wrote to please the one whom my soul loveth. The freedom to write without fear helped me become a better writer.

We win the internal struggle to allow ourselves to succeed through conquering limiting beliefs. Where did these beliefs come from, and how can I overcome them? I dig deeper into this subject in the next chapter. You may need a writing coach like myself to offer advice, guidance, and encouragement during your book's various stages.

As a last resort, if all else fails, or time is something you have very little of, you might want to look into a ghostwriter. As a ghostwriter, it saddens me to see the many who won't even try to write their books. Instead, they want it written for them. It seems like so many want instant gratification. The consequence is that they miss out on the journey. Before I agree to ghostwrite or coach, I ask clients and coachees to submit two to four paragraphs about their book to me in writing. Only after I see what they are capable of do I decide whether to help them or not. We are expensive, but many of us pour our hearts into our work.

After your final edit, print out your book. Go over it line by line and check for errors. While rewriting my drafts, I transition from proofreading to copy editing to make sure my book flows from start to finish. Over the years, I've become better at editing, with repetition, of course. I will still put this book in front of another pair of human eyes before I say it's complete. I also ask people I trust to read over my book; I want to make sure it is relevant. It helps to know what others think of your work. Again, beta readers or focus groups are an excellent way to get targeted feedback on your book. If you are planning a focus group, pay close attention to the marketing section. Determine who your ideal reader would be.

(Example: For this book, my ideal reader is an individual who wants to write a nonfiction book. They may be just starting, or maybe they are stuck. There's more to it, but you get what I am saying.)

Final caution, Be careful 'who' you let critique your book. Some people are dream killers. They may not see it for themselves; thus, they can't see it for you. Then you have those who, for whatever reason, will not want you to exceed them. In any case, guard the vision that God has given you. Don't let it get choked up in fear and doubt, but complete your work.

> *An anchor must hold you steady. When writing a book, you may not be in danger of the waves which break great ships into pieces, yet storms do rage in our lives. Don't let the fear of shipwreck make you loosen your anchor and sail away from your goals. Your anchor can hold against those thoughts that have swayed many souls from being authors."*

\- Ebony Lynnel Harris

Overcoming Self-Limiting Beliefs

Many have books they stopped writing because they experienced things that preprogram them to think negatively about themselves and others. I will include some examples from individuals I have worked with in the past.

In one of my workshops, a young man about nine years old said that his teacher told him he could not be a writer because he didn't know how to spell and use proper grammar. I responded, "I can barely spell myself, and that's why we have editors. They will help you as you go." I watched him turn from hopeless to hopeful in an instant. Friend, there are times when even those you look up to won't have faith in you; so believe in yourself. Now more on this grammar thing, you don't have to be perfect at grammar to write a book. Trust me, I know I just made someone cringe. I'm glad I put this at the end of the book. Textbooks written by professors need editing also because to err is human. Whether you are advanced or struggling, an editor is required. I don't know of any writers that don't make mistakes, which is why we have to rewrite our work repeatedly.

Writers can have learning challenges. They don't have to spend years writing to write an engaging book. I told one of my students, "If you can talk, you can write a book." Once you learn to construct a sentence, writing a book becomes easier. Most children learn to speak sentences before they can write their alphabet. You may have to have a book transcribed or have someone take dictation. It happens every day. While I'm on this subject, never let someone shame you because you didn't write your book in the same manner that they wrote theirs. All of us are individuals. Besides, your readers won't care as much about your methods as they do your message. Work on what you are going to say first. Make that the most important thing.

Another limiting belief is that your ideas aren't good enough. Why aren't your thoughts good? It's essential to not only look at what we say but why. You have to know within yourself that your ideas are just as good as anyone else's. Low self-worth can be disguised and leak out in occasional comments, usually when you don't expect it.

"Why would anyone read a book I wrote?" Lack of confidence stops so many from doing the things God called them to, the belief that they are not good enough. Our lives are books being read by all. If our lives are worthy of being recorded, can't we write something down to help someone along the way? You could have messed up big time, don't you think your story can help someone? That lesson wasn't just for you; we are helpers one to another.

To sum things up, the only way to overcome limiting beliefs is to take every thought captive. It sounds like a metaphor, but this is as literal as it gets. Imagine guards standing watch at the gates of a city, and the negative thoughts or intruders are trying to gain access. Your job is not to ignore but to identify the ideas trying to intrude and tell them that they are not welcome.

Examine yourself. If this thought keeps coming, are there any other thoughts already residing in you that may be connected? You may have welcomed them at once, but now, you have to revoke access, thus bringing into captivity every thought. Taking ideas captive requires you to always be on guard, which is not as exhausting as it sounds. You can do it, set up your mental bounty hunters, examine your thoughts, reevaluate how you view yourself, and overcome those limiting beliefs.

When you find those limiting beliefs, replace them with better ones. Start building yourself up, not in a proud way, but encouraging. Positive affirmations are an excellent way to reprogram your mind. My son and I listen to podcasts that are encouraging and uplifting, things that keep us motivated. Recently I had a day where I was feeling a little down. My son said, "Mom, how about we listen to Mr. Brown today." He pulled up Youtube and put on a video from Leslie Brown, and after listening, I was encouraged. Even I have to take thoughts captive. My prayer is that this book helps you write your book and gives you everything you need to be a successful writer.

> *"At the root of self-limiting beliefs is fear. Have you ever wondered why fear causes some to be paralyzed and feel powerless? I try to keep it at the forefront of my mind to give no place to fear and its torments. Thus, whenever fear enters, I speak first. It works out much better when the room isn't crowded."*
>
> - Ebony Lynnel Harris

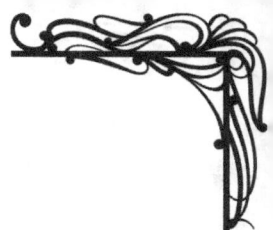

Another Way

I've heard it said, "If it's important, you will make time for it." While I believe these words wholeheartedly, there are some situations where this does not entirely apply. I found some people have the time; they lack the skills and ability to write. And others have so much going on, and time is not available to them. It's only 24 hours in a day, and sadly it is not always easy to find the time to take on such a task.

Sure, you can write outlines and even a draft for a short read like this in less than a day, but what happens if you have a longer, more in-depth book and lack the time or experience? Don't forget the hours of editing that goes into a book. Some have to attend to more important things. We cannot assume everyone has the same desires or even time and abilities. I believe anyone can write a book. It's hard to tell that to a person who can't see it for themselves.

Major bookstores have shelves filled with books from well-known celebrities and politicians. Many of them are only authors by name because they paid someone like myself to put in the long hours and write for them. Ghostwriting is an excellent option for someone who has a story to tell or valuable ideas but can't make it through the process I described.

Most people I work with know exactly what they want their book to say. They are busy professionals who can't take the time to slow down to write. If you lack time, I want you to know that ghostwrit-

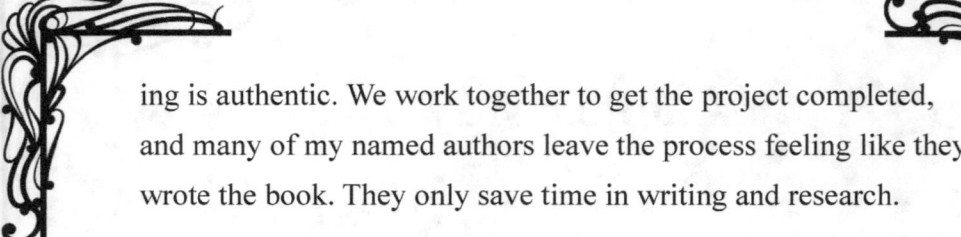

ing is authentic. We work together to get the project completed, and many of my named authors leave the process feeling like they wrote the book. They only save time in writing and research.

The Ready Writer

The ready writer has the necessary instruments for writing when inspiration comes. The tools can be a pen and paper or a laptop, voice recorder, dictionary, thesaurus, and a dedicated space to write. It may even be a cell phone. I can't tell you how many times I started typing in the notes app on my phone. The important thing is to write down the inspiration as it comes. Have you ever had a moment where you weren't writing, and inspiration came? Maybe you were in the middle of doing something important, what did you do? Listen, when you get inspired, you need to write it down before you lose it. I often say, "Treat inspiration like a visitor who rarely comes by. Make time for it. It's not like lightning. Inspiration often comes to the ready writer. It is hard to tell when certain thoughts will repeat."

One of the worst things is having an idea, I mean a good one, and to lose it. Some thoughts go as fast as they come, so make sure you value the inspiration that comes to you. How do you show that you value what came? You take the time to write it down. It takes less time to write your ideas down than it does to try and recount every thought looking for the revelation you lost, thoughts, and ideas that may never come again. There are two types of writers, the gifted and the skilled. Gifts come from God, and individuals need to practice to improve them. Anyone can obtain skills, and you need to practice to improve them. Whether you are gifted or want to acquire a skill, both require repetition to develop. Thus we see, writing is a skill that anyone can advance in if they are willing to keep working at it.

Imagine showing up every day after priming the pump of creativity over and over until the day when all you have to do is show up to a spring of inspiration flowing—books, poems, movies, plays, and many valuable ideas that can change the world. Friend, creatives aren't born, they show up daily when others are sleeping, and as a reward, inspiration meets them there. I didn't become an author and artist overnight. Over time, it happened through tests and trials, almost feeling like I wanted to throw in the towel, and after feeling like my ideas were complete failures. I had to endure the countless hours of editing and the pieces that I wrote that were too poor to share with the public. Each setback pushed me towards where I am today not that I am this great writer, but because I didn't give up, I can help someone else through their struggles. Give yourself time to grow. You can do this!

The Quest For Perfection

You want to be perfect. Everyone struggles with this, especially the new author. Some look at best selling authors and strive to be just like them. Before you strive for perfection, I say, strive to be 'Ready.' You still need to put in the long hours to rewrite and edit your book, don't wait too long. I've talked with individuals with books sitting for more than twenty years. What happens when your book sits too long? You grow as a person, and your content may no longer be relevant to you or your reader. Then you no longer have the attachment to the content that was initially there. Friend, if your book has been sitting that long, you may need to revamp it all together. Go in and take a fresh look at it. Can you still use the information that's in it? Chances are you can graze through taking the meat of it. The wording will almost always need to be changed.

How can a flawed individual write a perfect book? Even if you wrote a popular book, you would still have someone who goes against what you say. It's normal to want to write the best you can, and you can't please everyone. If you seek to please everyone, you will please no one. First-time authors need to give themselves time to grow. Don't compete with writers who have been at this longer than you existed. The competition would be internal anyway. At some point, you have to release your book.

In my opinion, the quest for perfection holds more would-be authors back than the lack of structure. Getting stuck can be dangerous for

the individual with writing goals. You know what to do, but this fear of failure and rejection pushes you to keep going at it from different angles until your book becomes obsolete or someone else gets the inspiration that initially came to you. Then you become the person sitting on the sidelines saying, "I thought about writing that book. It came to me years ago." Don't be that person. If you keep waiting for perfection, your book may never get published.

When inspiration comes, you need to act on it, move on time. The aim of the 'Ready Writer' is consistency, not perfection. Over time, you will grow as a writer. It is gratifying to look back on your work as it progresses. The writers' journey doesn't stop after their first book, and indeed you have more than one book in you. To the 'Ready Writer,' your journey as a writer will not be complete until you give out everything given to you. Only then can you say, "I've completed my task."

Marketing Your Book

Now is the perfect time to think about marketing. Make sure you are collecting names and have an audience to purchase your book. If your followers are not enough to help you reach your book goals, you can always use those purchases to gain reviews and ratings. While we are making a list, below are some other things to consider when marketing your book. Will you submit your text for traditional publishing, or will you self-publish? If you publish traditionally, there are strict word counts and book sizes you will have to keep in mind. If you decide to self-publish and wish to have your book in stores, there are other guidelines.

The last thing you want to do is have a book released without an audience or to have it created in a way that publishers and book stores won't accept. I worked for an author who had an excellent children's book. She submitted her work to a large chain store that said they wanted her book, but the size was off. I helped her get her book ready to be released in stores and learned that there were guidelines for getting your books in major stores. You would think that the policies are universal, but they aren't. They are unique to the various stores.

Friend, where do you want your book to go? If you plan to release your book in hardcopy or paperback, check the places you wish to have it and make sure you format it to the correct size. You will save a lot of time and money if you do it right the first time. Imagine getting an offer then having to pay to have changes done in a hurry.

Save yourself the headache. Below are the questions you want to use for marketing your book. Just as you created a profile for the reader when it's time, do one for your ideal customers. You want to include a visual.

What is their name, age, gender, or marital status?
What is their education level?
Where do they shop? Do they make online purchases?
What type of social media do they use, if any?
What is the average length book they read?
What do they do for entertainment?
Where do they purchase their books?
What forms of books do they read? (Digital, print, or audio)
What authors and genres do they enjoy?
What are some topics they are interested in reading?
(Create questions of your own.)

Do your clients prefer printed or electronic books? Knowing your customers can make this a more comfortable decision when choosing versions to have available for sale. If you have an online presence? You may want to test your audience and ask them some questions. If you are thinking about writing a book, now is an excellent time to start taking emails to keep your audience informed. Periodically, while working on your book, make sure you are letting your audience know what is coming. Keep those who follow you informed. If you are new to writing, start a blog or a podcast. Do something that will help you to gain and keep the attention of your future readers. Some authors reach out to influencers to get help with marketing their books. You may want to do the same.

When I help authors, I often use Facebook ads. Canva.com is an excellent way to design Facebook ads for those who are on a budget. Although you can find many free aids online to help you advertise your book, Facebook ads can bring a tremendous boost in your online sales, if done correctly.

> " *I wish I could tell you that I wake up every day inspired and ready to face the world. I don't, but I can't give up. I wish I could tell you that you won't have to go to the valley, but I can't. That's where you get your strength. When attempting to pitch your book idea or sell your book to potential customers, what do you do when you've dealt with rejection after rejection, and it seems like you can't get a break? You try one more time."*

- Ebony Lynnel Harris

Did the information in this book help you?

I want to know. Are you working on a book? Do you have any more concerns that need addressing? I may be able to explain it on my Facebook page. Thank you for your support. It is appreciated.

Join me online at lifetowords.com for a writing workshop. We go through children's stories, dissect them, play with them a little bit, then put them back together again. I have to warn you, we have fun, so if you're not accustomed to lots of laughs, brace yourself.

Connect with me on Social Media
Youtube: NoLimitLearning - Ebony Harris
Facebook: https://www.facebook.com/BePublishingCo/

Visit my online book store:
Faith2Faith Christian Bookstore: https://www.faith2faithbooks.com

> *Visions are important, and writing down your dream is an excellent place to start, but nothing will happen without having a plan to execute the idea. I challenge you to "make it plain." If you haven't done so already, write out how you plan to get from where you are to where you want to be."*
>
> *- Ebony Lynnel Harris*

About The Author

My name is Ebony, and I am a writer. It sounds like I'm about to introduce myself as an addict. I am, not that I roam the street looking for substances to fill a void, but I have this desire to write that I cannot avoid; If I were to hold it in, I fear it would be like fire. Inspiration running through my mind, then I have this duty to write my wrongs out for all to see, full transparency. I aim to create content that stimulates the mind, inspiring you to flow as you grow until you can eventually sow into the life of another.

Not only am I an author and artist, but I am also a ghostwriter and writing coach who formerly taught storytelling to youth in Baltimore City.

"If creative writing were contagious, I'd aim to infect everyone I come in contact with, education = duplication."
- Ebony Lynnel Harris.

In 2013, I started working to help youth in Baltimore City set goals towards their future. In an environment where many feel hopeless, my goal is to help someone believe that better days are coming for them. I also helped writers of all ages to become published authors. After teaching for some time, I've learned that the lack of experience is not the only thing that holds individuals back from becoming authors.

In the past, I became stagnant because of discouragement. 'What if' I let it stop me? Many would not be authors today. This 'what if' drives me to help individuals set goals towards their future and tell their stories. Some only need a push in the right direction, some encouragement along the way, and then some require you to hold their hand and walk them through the process. Friend, if you are in a struggle to write, I've been where you are. Let me help you wherever you may be.

More From Ebony Harris

THE PURSUIT OF WISDOM | JOURNAL SERIES

In today's world of social distancing, the need for connection rings louder than ever. BE Publishing Co. has a series of prayer journals designed to launch the journaler into a deeper walk with God. For those experienced journalers, we recognize that one page may not be enough to write your daily entries, so our journal, "The Pursuit of Wisdom", has plenty of space for writing. This journal is designed with wisdom scriptures at the top of each page which makes it easier to hide the Word Of God in your heart. Use the spaces provided for anything you like: Reflections, Thanksgiving, Scriptures, Devotions, Gratitude, Prayers, Poetry, Drawings, and more.

Our lives are much more demanding with distanced learning and so many other things. I encourage you to incorporate prayer journaling into your daily routine for the whole family. Start a new norm, along with all the other ones that started this year. Meditate on the scriptures, listen to the voice of God, pray and then allow Him to direct your pathways. Wisdom is still crying out in the streets. Pursue it!

THE FAITH-2-FAITH LINED JOURNAL SERIES

I am an advocate for daily writing. Yes, it is because of our consistency that we develop our craft. Writing is about more than producing a book or poem. It provides therapy on so many levels. Oh, that you would experience the joys of daily writing. These journals are perfect for men, women, or teenage girls and boys. Have you ever wondered why other writers seem to pass you by while you're at a standstill? You think, "This is my season to wait. I will sit here and wait for inspiration to hit me." or "I'm not as good as they are, so, why should I bother?" Could it be that inspiration comes to the ready writer? The writer who decides to write whether they are inspired or not. Why does it seem like some people are more creative than others? It's because some people struggle with inconsistency. If you aren't faithfully working on the little things, how can you be trusted with the overflow? We want to be inspired so that ideas never stop coming, but what are we doing with the inspiration that does come to us? Start writing daily today! These decorated journals with lines have 240-pages and are available exclusively on www.faith2faithbooks.com. These journals will definitely be useful for all your writing needs.

As Christian authors we write like our readers lives depend on it, because it does.

Are you a self-published Christian author looking to get your book on the FAITH2FAITH Online Christian Bookstore?

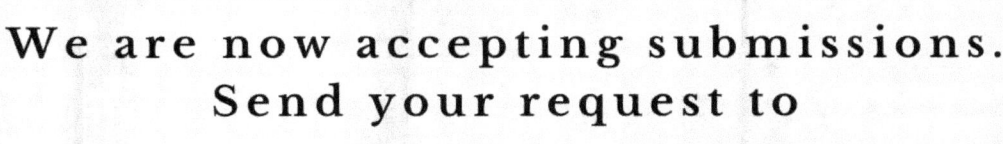

We are now accepting submissions. Send your request to submissions@faith2faithbooks.com

www.ingramcontent.com/pod-product-compliance
Lightning Source LLC
Chambersburg PA
CBHW072023110526
44592CB00012B/1408